david carr glover

SCALE BOOK

scales

triads and inversions

cadence chords

in all the major and minor keys

for piano

ISBN 978-0-7935-2571-3

G. SCHIRMER, Inc.

DISTRIBUTED BY

HAL•LEONARD®
CORPORATION

7777 W. BLUEMOUND RD. P.O. BOX 13819 MILWAUKEE, WI 53213

The chords and progressions as presented in this book will prepare students for the Intermediate Class auditions of the National Guild of Piano Teachers.

Whole (1) and Half (½) Steps of the Major and Minor Scales

Steps of the Major Scale

Steps of the Natural Minor Scale

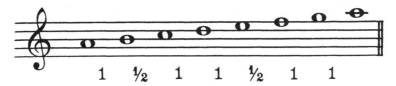

Steps of the Harmonic Minor Scale

Steps of the Melodic Minor Scale

C MAJOR
(Relative to A minor)

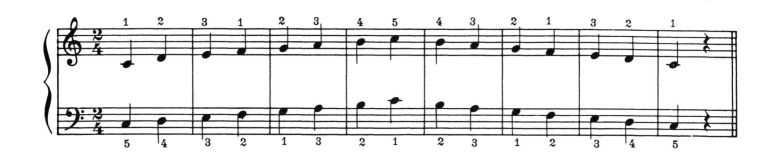

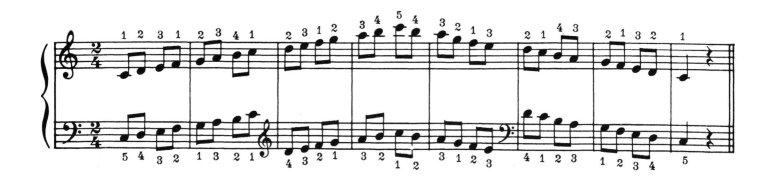

TRIADS AND INVERSIONS

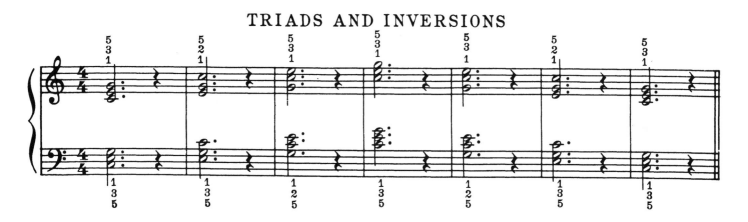

CADENCE CHORDS

A MINOR
(Relative to C Major)

A NATURAL MINOR

*A HARMONIC MINOR

TRIADS AND INVERSIONS

CADENCE CHORDS

* Melodic Minor Scales will be found on pages **32, 33** and **34**.

G MAJOR - KEY SIGNATURE F♯

(Relative to E minor)

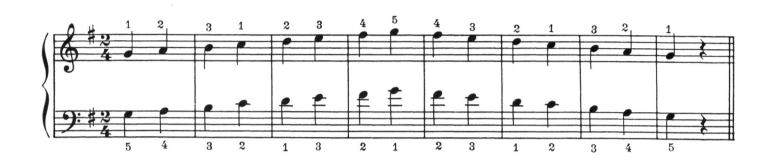

TRIADS AND INVERSIONS

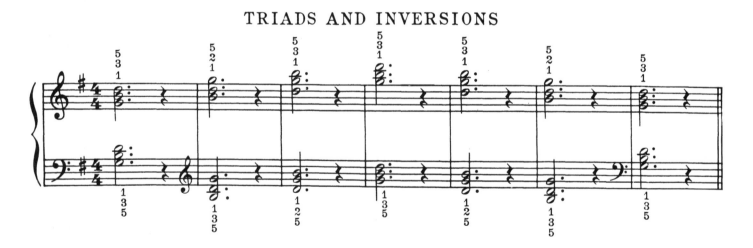

CADENCE CHORDS

E MINOR- KEY SIGNATURE F#
(Relative to G Major)

E NATURAL MINOR

E HARMONIC MINOR

TRIADS AND INVERSIONS

CADENCE CHORDS

Em Am Em B Em

I   IV I   V I

D MAJOR - KEY SIGNATURE F♯ C♯
(Relative to B minor)

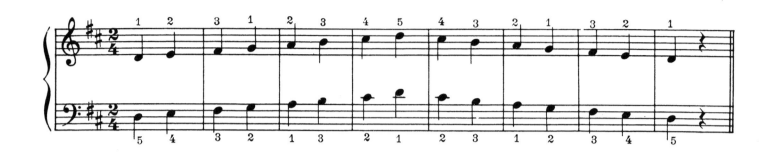

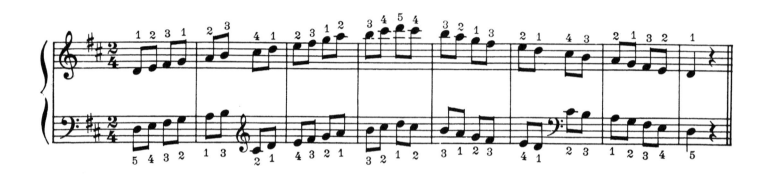

TRIADS AND INVERSIONS

CADENCE CHORDS

B MINOR- KEY SIGNATURE F# C#

(Relative to D Major)

B NATURAL MINOR

B HARMONIC MINOR

TRIADS AND INVERSIONS

CADENCE CHORDS

A MAJOR - KEY SIGNATURE F♯ C♯ G♯

(Relative to F♯ minor)

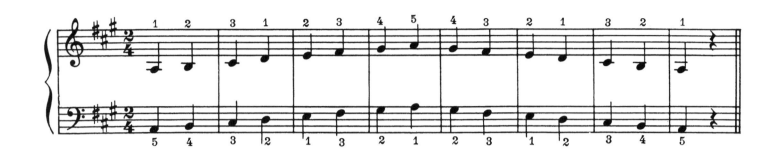

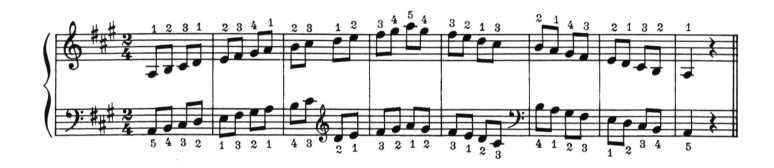

TRIADS AND INVERSIONS

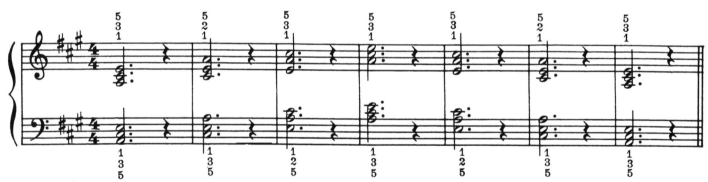

CADENCE CHORDS

F# MINOR - KEY SIGNATURE F# C# G#

(Relative to A Major)

F# NATURAL MINOR

F# HARMONIC MINOR

TRIADS AND INVERSIONS

CADENCE CHORDS

F#m Bm F#m C# F#m

I   IV   I   V   I

E MAJOR-KEY SIGNATURE F♯ C♯ G♯ D♯

(Relative to C♯ minor)

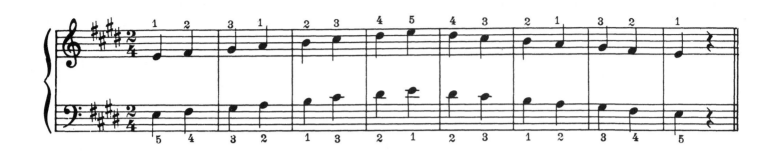

TRIADS AND INVERSIONS

CADENCE CHORDS

C♯ MINOR - KEY SIGNATURE F♯ C♯ G♯ D♯

(Relative to E Major)

B MAJOR - KEY SIGNATURE F# C# G# D# A#

(Relative to G# minor)
(Enharmonic to Cb Major)

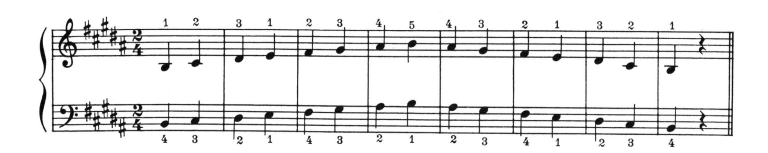

TRIADS AND INVERSIONS

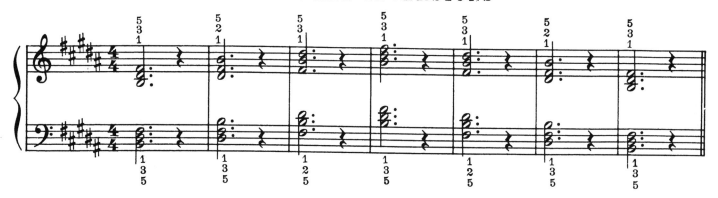

CADENCE CHORDS

G♯ MINOR-KEY SIGNATURE F♯ C♯ G♯ D♯ A♯

(Relative to B Major)
(Enharmonic to A♭ minor)

G♯ NATURAL MINOR

G♯ HARMONIC MINOR

TRIADS AND INVERSIONS

CADENCE CHORDS

F♯ MAJOR-KEY SIGNATURE F♯ C♯ G♯ D♯ A♯ E♯

(Relative to D♯ minor)
(Enharmonic to G♭ Major)

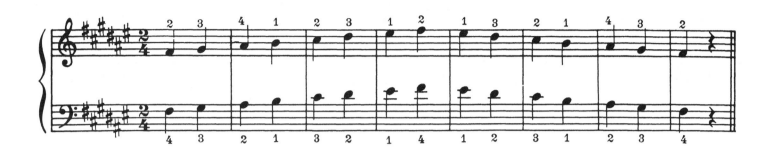

TRIADS AND INVERSIONS

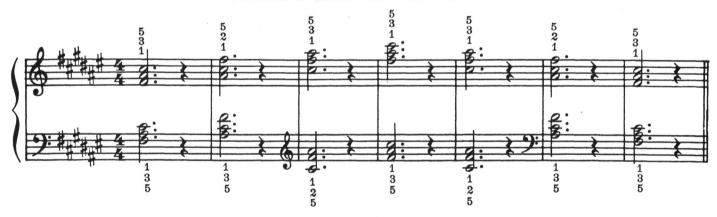

CADENCE CHORDS

D# MINOR - KEY SIGNATURE F# C# G# D# A# E#

(Relative to F# Major)
(Enharmonic to Eb minor)

D# NATURAL MINOR

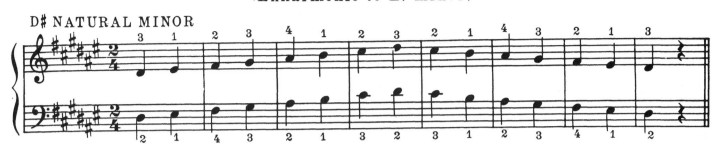

D# HARMONIC MINOR

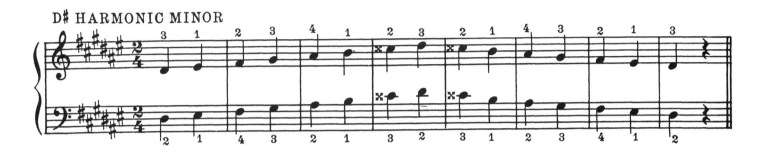

TRIADS AND INVERSIONS

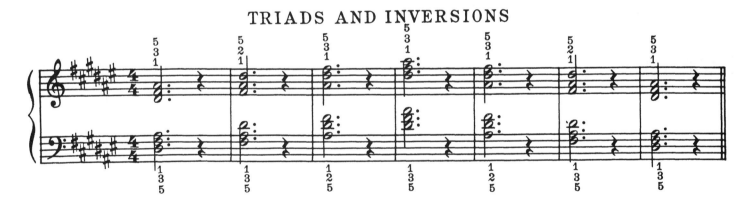

CADENCE CHORDS

I   IV   I   V   I

C♯ MAJOR-KEY SIGNATURE F♯ C♯ G♯ D♯ A♯ E♯ B♯

(Relative to A♯ minor)
(Enharmonic to D♭ Major)

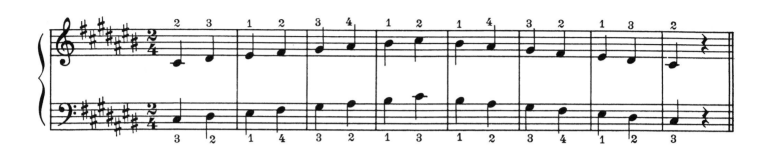

TRIADS AND INVERSIONS

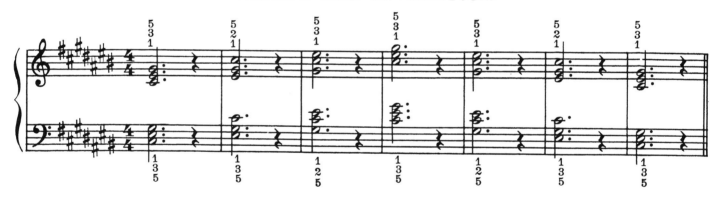

CADENCE CHORDS

A♯ MINOR - KEY SIGNATURE F♯ C♯ G♯ D♯ A♯ E♯ B♯

(Relative to C♯ Major)
(Enharmonic to B♭ minor)

A♯ NATURAL MINOR

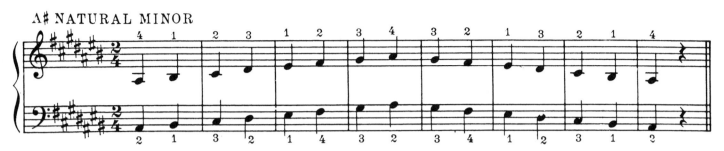

A♯ HARMONIC MINOR

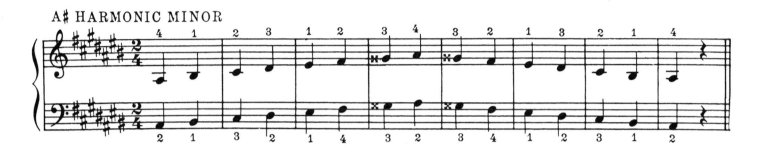

TRIADS AND INVERSIONS

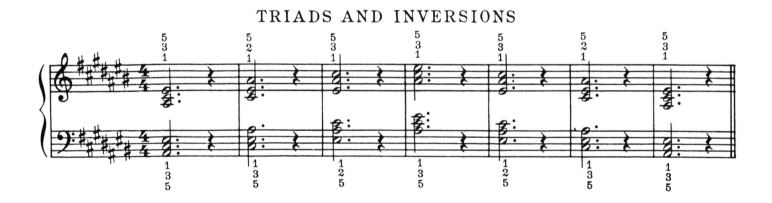

CADENCE CHORDS

A♯m D♯m A♯m E♯ A♯m

I   IV   I   V   I

F MAJOR - KEY SIGNATURE B♭
(Relative to D minor)

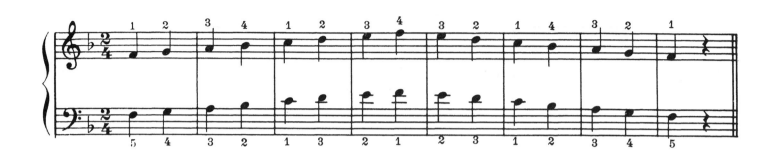

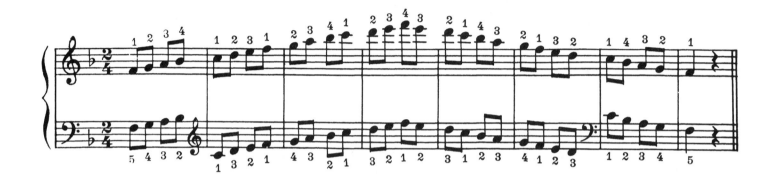

TRIADS AND INVERSIONS

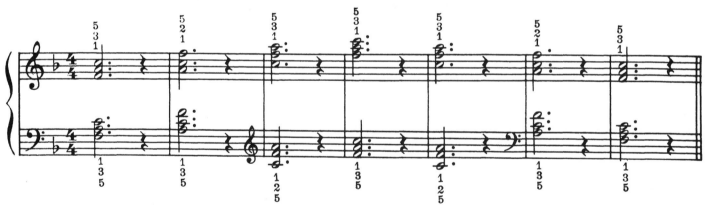

CADENCE CHORDS

D MINOR - KEY SIGNATURE B♭
(Relative to F Major)

D NATURAL MINOR

D HARMONIC MINOR

TRIADS AND INVERSIONS

CADENCE CHORDS

Dm Gm Dm A Dm

I IV I V I

B♭ MAJOR-KEY SIGNATURE B♭ E♭

(Relative to G minor)

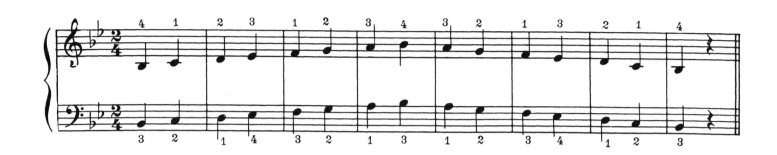

TRIADS AND INVERSIONS

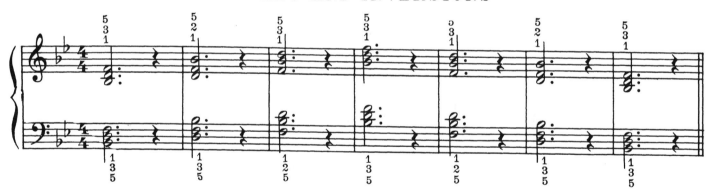

CADENCE CHORDS

G MINOR - KEY SIGNATURE B♭ E♭

(Relative to B♭ Major)

G NATURAL MINOR

G HARMONIC MINOR

TRIADS AND INVERSIONS

CADENCE CHORDS

Gm Cm Gm D Gm

I IV I V I

E♭ MAJOR-KEY SIGNATURE B♭ E♭ A♭

(Relative to C minor)

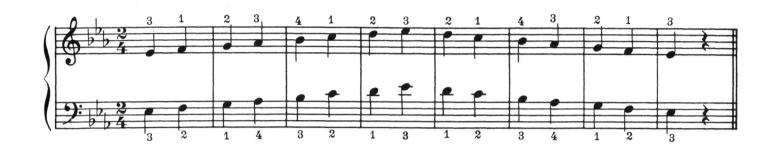

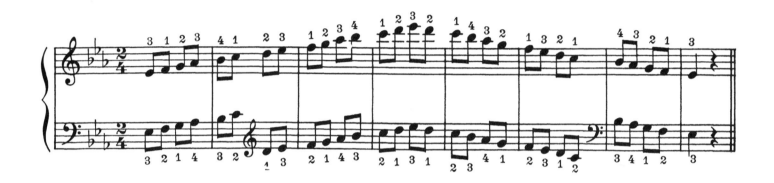

TRIADS AND INVERSIONS

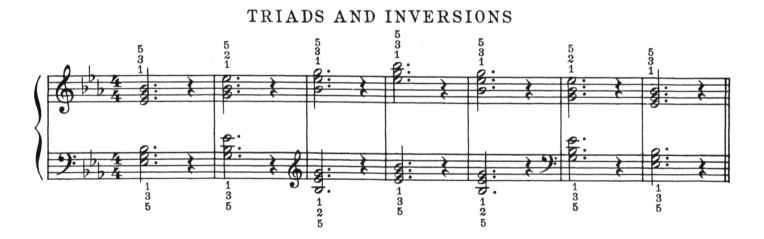

CADENCE CHORDS

C MINOR- KEY SIGNATURE B♭ E♭ A♭
(Relative to E♭ Major)

C NATURAL MINOR

C HARMONIC MINOR

TRIADS AND INVERSIONS

CADENCE CHORDS

Cm Fm Cm G   Cm

I   IV   I   V   I

A♭ MAJOR- KEY SIGNATURE B♭E♭A♭D♭

(Relative to F minor)

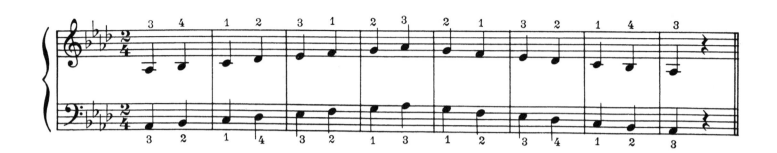

TRIADS AND INVERSIONS

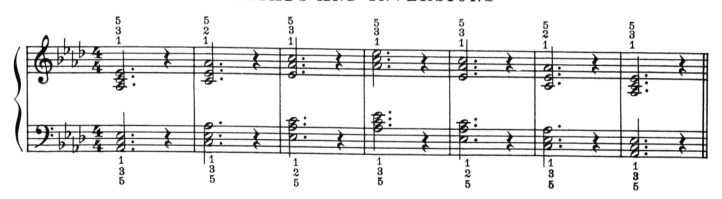

CADENCE CHORDS

F MINOR-KEY SIGNATURE B♭E♭A♭D♭
(Relative to A♭ Major)

F NATURAL MINOR

F HARMONIC MINOR

TRIADS AND INVERSIONS

CADENCE CHORDS

Fm B♭m Fm C Fm

I   IV   I   V   I

D♭ MAJOR - KEY SIGNATURE B♭ E♭ A♭ D♭ G♭

(Relative to B♭ minor)
(Enharmonic to C♯ Major)

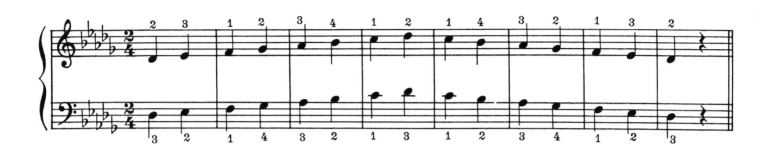

TRIADS AND INVERSIONS

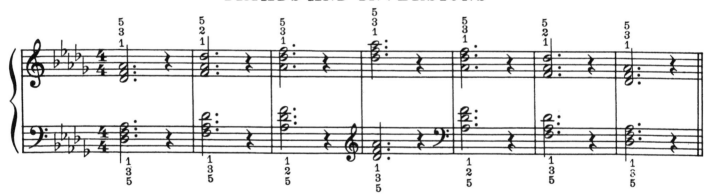

CADENCE CHORDS

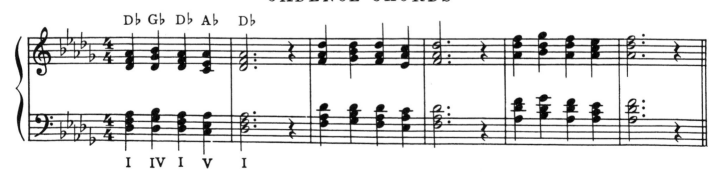

B♭ MINOR- KEY SIGNATURE B♭E♭A♭D♭G♭

(Relative to D♭ Major)
(Enharmonic to A♯ minor)

B♭ NATURAL MINOR

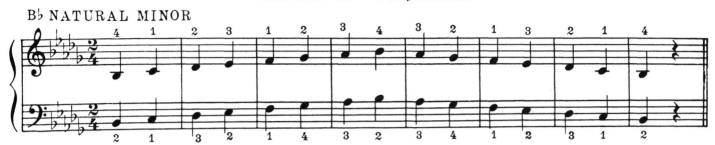

B♭ HARMONIC MINOR

TRIADS AND INVERSIONS

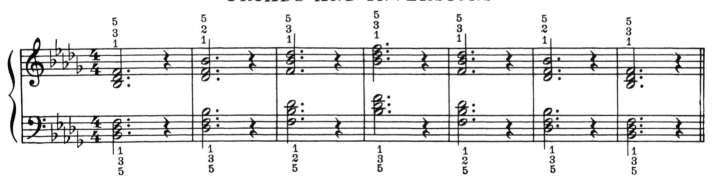

CADENCE CHORDS

G♭ MAJOR - KEY SIGNATURE B♭ E♭ A♭ D♭ G♭ C♭

(Relative to E♭ minor)

(Enharmonic to F♯ Major)

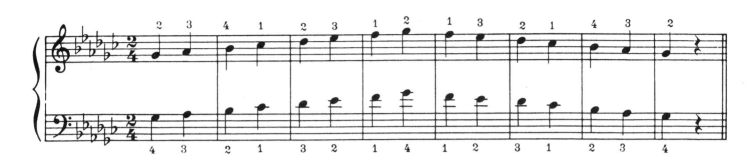

TRIADS AND INVERSIONS

CADENCE CHORDS

G♭ C♭ G♭ D♭ G♭

I IV I V I

E♭ MINOR-KEY SIGNATURE B♭E♭A♭D♭G♭C♭

(Relative to G♭ Major)
(Enharmonic to D♯ minor)

E♭ NATURAL MINOR

E♭ HARMONIC MINOR

TRIADS AND INVERSIONS

CADENCE CHORDS

Cb MAJOR - KEY SIGNATURE Bb Eb Ab Db Gb Cb Fb

(Relative to Ab minor)

(Enharmonic to B Major)

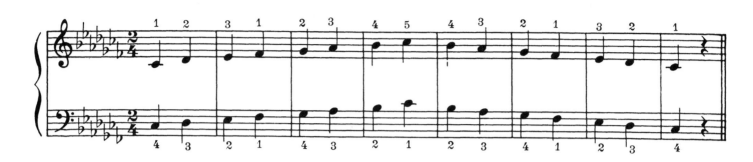

TRIADS AND INVERSIONS

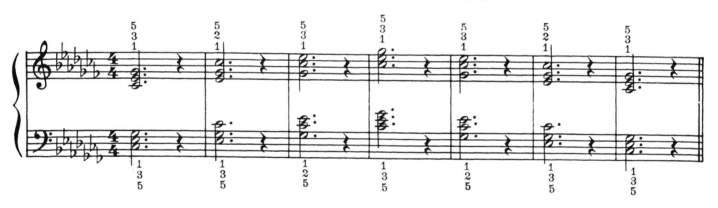

CADENCE CHORDS

Cb Fb Cb Gb Cb

I IV I V I

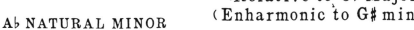

A♭ MINOR-KEY SIGNATURE B♭ E♭ A♭ D♭ G♭ C♭ F♭

(Relative to C♭ Major)
(Enharmonic to G♯ minor)

A♭ NATURAL MINOR

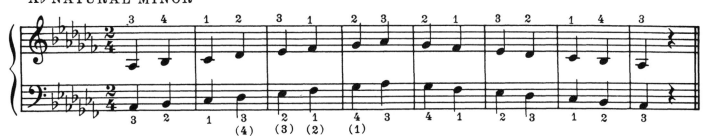

A♭ HARMONIC MINOR

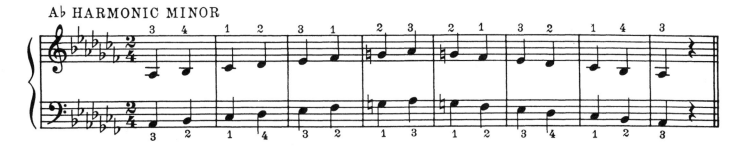

TRIADS AND INVERSIONS

CADENCE CHORDS

A♭m D♭m A♭m E♭ A♭m

I IV I V I

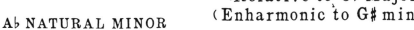

G# MELODIC MINOR (Enharmonic to Ab minor)
Relative to B Major

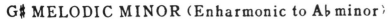

D# MELODIC MINOR (Enharmonic to Eb minor)
Relative to F# Major

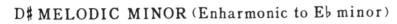

A# MELODIC MINOR (Enharmonic to Bb minor)
Relative to C# Major

D MELODIC MINOR
Relative to F Major

G MELODIC MINOR
Relative to Bb Major

34

C MELODIC MINOR
Relative to E♭ Major

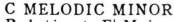

F MELODIC MINOR
Relative to A♭ Major

B♭ MELODIC MINOR (Enharmonic to A♯ minor)
Relative to D♭ Major

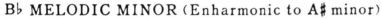

E♭ MELODIC MINOR (Enharmonic to D♯ minor)
Relative to G♭ Major

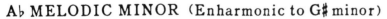

A♭ MELODIC MINOR (Enharmonic to G♯ minor)
Relative to C♭ Major